THE HEYDAY OF THE BUS: YORKSHIRE

GEOFF LUMB

IAN ALLAN
Publishing

First published 1996

ISBN 0 7110 2445 6

Published by Ian Allan Publishing
an imprint of Ian Allan Ltd, Terminal House,
Station Approach, Shepperton, Surrey TW17 8AS.
Printed by Ian Allan Printing Ltd, Coombelands House,
Coombelands Lane, Addlestone, Surrey KT15 1HY.

Front Cover:

An Intruder
Halifax purchased its first Leyland, a TS2 Tiger
single-deck bus in late 1929 for the Corporation 'A'
fleet, followed by its one and only Dennis EV
single-deck bus in January 1930. After this, all
purchases for the 'A' fleet and the 'B' Joint Omnibus
Committee fleet were AECs until 1939 when two
Leyland Cubs with 20-seat Park Royal bodies
arrived. These lasted for only 12 months before
transfer on loan to the LNER. Halifax was one of the
few corporations not to receive any wartime buses.
Its first postwar buses were eight London-type RT3
AEC Regents in late 1946 for the 'A' fleet. Large
numbers of Provincial Regals and Regents were
ordered for both 'A' and 'B' fleets. However, before
these arrived, Leyland quickly supplied nine of the
new Leyland Titan PD2/1 double-deck buses with
Leyland bodies, the first entering service in October
1947. ACP 390 arrived in November 1947 as fleet
number 341. In 1952 it was renumbered 106. It is
seen entering West Vale and survived in service
until 1966, outliving many of the later AECs and the
1951 Daimler CD650s.
V. Nutton, Courtesy G. Lumb Collection

Back cover:

Well, it's a new Registration!
In 1934 a joint company was formed to merge the
York Corporation Transport Department with the
local services in the York area of the West Yorkshire
Road Car Co Ltd, known as York-West Yorkshire
Joint Committee. In 1955, 11 prewar Bristol K5G
double-deck buses used as York Y379-399 were
rebuilt as new vehicles, fitted with new chassis
sides and new ECW high-bridge bodies seating 55
or 56. They were renumbered YDG82–92 and re-
registered OWT 195–205. YDG85 is seen outside the
city walls at York railway station in October
1964. *G. Lumb*

Introduction

Yorkshire was the largest county in England
before the 1974 local government
reorganisation. It has been said that 'there
are as many acres in Yorkshire as there are
words in the Bible'. Divided into three
Ridings, it was a county of contrasts.

From the densely populated industrial
areas in the West Riding (now split between
South and West Yorkshire) to the remote
rural Dales, Yorkshire extended westwards
to within eight miles of Morecambe Bay and
the Irish Sea. To the east of the low-lying
central plain which stretched northwards
from Selby to the Vale of York were the
coastal resorts of Bridlington, Filey and
Scarborough. Yorkshire was bounded in the
north by the industrial conurbation of
Teesside, where the River Tees formed a
boundary with County Durham, and in the
south by the Humber Estuary, separating the
ports of Hull and Goole from Lincolnshire.

The network of bus services which
covered Yorkshire were operated by
municipalities, BET and Tilling group
companies along with dozens of
independents, large and small, in between.

One such independent was Mr Noble's
Forge Valley Motors, which operated
between Scarborough and Langdale End.
When I travelled on his utility Bedford bus in
1951 the fare was paid as you left the bus and
despite having tickets in a rack, I never saw
the driver issue any of them. Mr Noble
continued to make a meagre living until the
summer of 1961 when the service was taken
over by United.

At the other end of the county, one could
see an endless procession of double-deck
buses running through the Don Valley past
the many steel works which lay between
Sheffield and Rotherham, carrying the
hundreds of shift workers.

Many of the municipalities operated joint
services with their neighbours and a
surprising number of other municipalities
operated into Yorkshire from adjoining
counties, not all arriving by road. West
Hartlepool used the Tees Transporter Bridge
to carry its buses into Middlesbrough.

Yorkshire was also unique in that during
1929–1930, the railways reached agreement
with five municipalities to operate buses
jointly, the five being Halifax, Huddersfield,
Leeds, Sheffield and Todmorden. A further
municipality, Rochdale in Lancashire, had
its service to Halifax taken over by the LMS
Railway. The introduction of the 1930 Road
Traffic Act in January 1931 to regulate bus
services nullified many of the railway
powers as all services now came under the
control of Traffic Commissioners, who were
responsible for regulating their operation.
The agreement between the LMS and LNE
Railways and Leeds Corporation — effective
from April 1929 with 23 buses in the Leeds
'B' fleet jointly owned — was terminated in
July 1931 when Leeds refused to surrender
tram routes in the joint 'B' fleet area when
running of these routes was surrendered or
abandoned.

The 1930 Road Traffic Act established
patterns of services which continued
through to the 1950s when the decline in
usage of buses started to affect rural areas
and many small operators ceased to run
sparsely-used services, and even larger
companies withdrew unprofitable services
in some cases, allowing smaller companies
to take them over.

As more and more people purchased
motor cars and television sets, the number of
operators with stage-carriage services was
reduced by 50% between 1954 and 1979.

The heyday of the Yorkshire bus was in
the postwar years before the decline in the
1960s when local authorities had to give
financial support in the form of operator
subsidies to ensure that some services were
continued. A similar pattern was also
evident in the unremunerative services
operated by the various municipalities, with
many fringe services being withdrawn. At
the same time, the remaining tramway and
trolleybus operators in Yorkshire substituted

motor-buses as replacements. When Dr Beeching axed many of the remaining branch railway lines, replacement bus services were introduced where the existing bus network failed to serve some of the communities deprived of the railway. Many of these replacement bus services were withdrawn after a period due to lack of support.

Some of the municipalities had general managers who, faced with rising costs, pioneered changes. One of these was at Huddersfield where to effect economies, special dispensation was obtained in 1951 to operate 43-seat one man operated buses. The limit at that time for one man operated buses was 29 seats.

To benefit from and take advantage of the changes in vehicle size and to effect other economies, some of the Yorkshire BET companies replaced fairly new 32-seat single-deck buses with new 45-seat ones. The displaced 32-seat buses had their bodies removed before new double-deck bodies were fitted to the refurbished chassis, thus improving the fleet at minimum expense. Other single-deck vehicles purchased in 1950 were lengthened in 1955 from 27ft 6in to 30ft, increasing their seating capacity from 32 to 38. However, they were still unsuitable for one man operation unless when used as a 'duplicate car' to the longer stage-carriage or express services where only one conductor would travel in the convoy, usually in the service car or coach. These vehicles on lengthening were painted in coach livery. In 1962, most of these, displaced by new 53-seat single-deck buses in coach livery, were then rebuilt a second time, this time having new forward-entrance double-deck bodies fitted.

Some of the independents, like Hansons, rebuilt earlier coach chassis, fitting new single or double-deck bus bodies. So in 1969 when Huddersfield Corporation purchased the Hanson bus service, only three of the vehicles had been bought new as buses.

One of the problems with rebuilt and rebodied vehicles was the Motor Taxation Department of the local authority.

Dewsbury, Huddersfield, Leeds and Wakefield insisted on the vehicle keeping its original registration number. When County Motors (Lepton) Ltd rebuilt two Leyland PS1 single-deck buses, having new Roe double-deck bodies fitted, they could not have new Huddersfield registration numbers, so they were transferred to Yorkshire Traction and given new Barnsley CB (County Borough) registration numbers and repainted into Yorkshire Traction livery.

Hansons found a way round this by allocating a new chassis number to each vehicle, the sequence starting at 6666 which was the Hanson telephone number. West Yorkshire Road Car had the same problem with their rebodied vehicles, only one batch at York having new West Riding County Council registration numbers.

All this was a long time before the DVLA at Swansea, cherished number plates, and the use of Northern Ireland registrations to disguise the age of the vehicles.

Not all operators refurbished existing vehicles. The largest independent, West Riding Automobile at Wakefield, persuaded Guy Motors to produce the Wulfrunian, which was revolutionary in concept having full air suspension and disc brakes, but was to be costly to maintain.

Some services linked obscure villages with a major town or city, filling in gaps left by the larger companies, such as the marathon run from Rawmarsh to Leeds operated by T. Burrows of Wombwell who survived until November 1966 when his service was taken over jointly by West Riding Automobile Co and the Yorkshire Traction Co.

After the October 1964 general election had given Britain a Labour government for the first time since 1951, the new Government addressed the problems affecting public transport and after the appointment in late 1965 of Barbara Castle as the new Minister of Transport much thought went into finding solutions. In the 1966 White Paper proposals it was suggested that essential rural bus services should receive public money and that regional transport

boards would cover the entire country. These proposals led to the BET group selling its bus and coach interests to the British Transport Commission and the amalgamation with the Tilling companies to form the National Bus Co.

Where the different companies overlapped, rationalisation followed with companies in Yorkshire like Hebble, County and Mexborough & Swinton being merged with others. The largest independent, West Riding, was sold to the National Bus Co.

Other companies like Ledgards, Farsley and Kippax, fearing the regional transport boards, sold out to others. Whilst Huddersfield paved the way with the repurchase of the railway interest and then took over Hansons, Todmorden disappeared into a new Calderdale Joint Omnibus Committee.

So the scene was set for the 1974 changes in local government when the West Yorkshire PTE and the South Yorkshire PTE were formed to take over the West Riding municipalities.

The photographs in this album have been selected to give the reader a pictorial tour around Yorkshire in the 1960s when one could see an enormous variety of vehicles, from the standardised vehicles in the Tilling fleets to the unusual and special vehicles which were 'tailor-made' for specific services.

I hope that you enjoy the tour and that you are not too disappointed if your favourite vehicle or operator is not included in my choice.

G. Lumb
Huddersfield
November 1995

Title page:
Any more for Darrowby!
Percival Bros (Coaches) Ltd operated services up Swaledale. In June 1966, Bedford RHN 107 is waiting for passengers for Reeth, Gunnerside, Muker and Keld – an area featured many years later in the films and TV series about 'James Herriot' the creation of Thirsk vet, Alfred White, who died in 1995. *G. Lumb*

Above:
An Unusual Combination
Middlesbrough Corporation No 77, one of 10 Guy Arab III buses with ECW bodies which entered service in 1950, is seen loading with Middlesbrough football supporters in September 1963 when the fare was 4d (less than 2p!).

6   *G. Lumb*

Right:
Low Bridge Solution
For services where the station's low bridge restricted headroom, Middlesbrough purchased nine Dennis Lolines, eight in 1960 with forward-entrance Northern Counties bodies. The other one was No 99, a 1958 mark I with a 67-seat rear-entrance Northern Counties body. *G. Lumb*

Above:

Trams to Buses

In 1921 Middlesbrough and Stockton Corporations purchased the Teesside interests of the Imperial Tramways which included a through tram route from Norton to North Ormesby via Stockton, Thornaby and Middlesbrough. In 1931 it was replaced by motorbuses provided by both corporations. This 1960 view shows Stockton No 6, a 1954 Leyland-bodied Leyland motorbus waiting to leave North Ormesby for Norton in County Durham. *G. Lumb*

Above:
Trolleybus Feeders

Teesside Railless Traction Board was formed in 1919 by Middlesbrough Corporation (⅓) and Eston Urban District Council (⅔) to operate trolleybuses between North Ormesby and Normanby with a branch to Grangetown. In 1926, motorbuses were introduced as feeders to the trolleybuses. This 1963 view shows No 22, a 1957 Leyland PD2/20, and No 29, a 1963 Leyland PD2A/27, both being fitted with Roe-built bodies. The slatted grilles above the driver's cab show that in both cases Cave-Brown-Cave heating systems are fitted.
G. Lumb

9

Right:
Miniature Railway Operator
Saltburn Motor Services Ltd had a network of services, linking Saltburn with Loftus and Guisborough as well as many workmen's services, to the steel works on Teesside South Bank. This 1967 view shows one of two Burlingham-bodied Leyland Tiger Cubs purchased from Wilkinson Motor Services, Sedgefield in late 1964. TPT 448 is returning to Saltburn in July 1967 with the then closed ironworks at Skinningrove in the background. SMS also owned and operated a ¾-mile-long 15in gauge miniature railway in the Valley Gardens, at Saltburn. *G. Lumb*

Right:
Problems with Hills
The principal company operator in Cleveland and North Yorkshire was United Automobile Services Ltd. This view shows the difficult operating territory where, in the interests of safety, United used roadside notices to advise drivers how to climb or descend that particular hill. This ensured that drivers would not attempt to change gear whilst on that hill. A 1962 Bristol MW6G (UE 544) is seen in 1971 climbing out of Goathland, now made famous as Aidensfield in the TV programme 'Heartbeat' on its way to Whitby. The author remembers in 1953 having to get off and walk up this hill with other fit and able passengers when on a ½-day excursion from Redcar to Goathland. The prewar Bristol with five-cylinder engine would not climb it fully laden, an example of the Tilling Group's policy of fuel economy being more important than power output. *G. Lumb*

Above:
Hill Climbing Solution
In 1950 when United purchased NHN 121 it was a Bristol LL5G with 39-seat ECW body. Built at Irthlingborough, it was also one of the first United 30ft-long buses. In 1954 it was converted to type LL6B by the fitting of a Bristol six-cylinder engine and reseated with 32 express seats. It was repainted into a cream and red livery with additional beading — and could climb the hills around Whitby with passengers and luggage. In late 1960 it was converted back to 39 seats and repainted into red and cream bus livery. This 1964 view shows it at Whitby with the additional beading still evident.
V. Nutton, Courtesy G. Lumb Collection

Left:
Promenade Buses
In 1957 for the Scarborough seafront service, United rebuilt and lengthened earlier Bristol L5G buses to become model LL5G, fitting them with special 8ft-wide centre-entrance bodies seating 39 which were built by ECW and resembled the full-fronted coach bodies built for vertical-engined chassis. BGS 5 is shown at the North Bay terminus in August 1964.
G. Lumb

Above:
Scarborough Independent
Seen loading at the Westwood coach station, Scarborough is Hardwicks Services Ltd 1953 Leyland-bodied Leyland RUA 294. In 1952 Hardwicks was purchased by Wallace Arnold Tours Ltd, the Leeds coaching company, with RUA 294 being the first new vehicle to be provided by the new owner. Note that the roof is painted red only at the front and rear domes. Platform doors have been fitted for the long journey to Ebberston. *V. Nutton, Courtesy G. Lumb Collection*

Above:
Trunk Route Duplicate Cars
A selection of East Yorkshire Motor Services Ltd being used as duplicates to Hull from Scarborough. The leading vehicle is No 616, a 1953 Leyland Royal Tiger with rear-entrance Windover coach body.

14   *V. Nutton, Courtesy G. Lumb Collection*

Right:
Cherry Picked
Local services in Beverley were provided by Cherry Coaches who had purchased HUF 270, a former Southdown Motor Services 1947 Windover-bodied Leyland Tiger.
G. Lumb

Left:
Hull Joint
East Yorkshire Motor Services Ltd had a number of services operated jointly with Hull Corporation. No 493, a 1950 Leyland PD1A, carried a 54-seat Roe highbridge body to Beverley Bar profile. *G. Lumb*

Above:
Independent to Spurn
Also to be seen in Hull on its service to Easington was Connor & Grahams Ltd Leyland Royal Tiger MRR 987 built in 1951 with a Yeates 41-seat coach body. *G. Lumb*

17

Above:

Stop-gap Purchase

Kingston-upon-Hull Corporation Transport operated both trolleybuses and motorbuses, the trolleybuses being withdrawn between 1961 and 1964 and replaced by new motorbuses. To replace wartime vehicles which were life expired, the Corporation purchased many second-hand motorbuses from Newcastle, St Helens and Nottingham. Daimler CVG6 No 128 (KVK 970) was one of 10 buses purchased from Newcastle Corporation in 1961. The body had been built by Metro-Cammell to Birmingham City Transport specification. *G. Lumb*

Above:
West Riding Port
The other Yorkshire port on the Humber Estuary was Goole in the West Riding.
In 1964, FBU 915, a Duple-bodied Bedford OB, was owned by Yorkshire &

Lincolnshire Road Services Ltd, Swinefleet, who operated two services from
Goole to Scunthorpe and Gainsborough until May 1967 when Lincolnshire
Road Car Co Ltd took them over.
G. Lumb

Left:
Goole Local
Ben Sketcher, also from Swinefleet, was operating GBE 848, a forward control 1950 Bedford OB with Plaxton body, on his service to Crowle from Goole in 1964. In April 1967, Lincolnshire Road Car Co Ltd took the service over. *G. Lumb*

Above:
Goole Town
In 1964, some of the Goole Town services were already operated by Lincolnshire Road Car Co Ltd. Typical of the Road Car Co's fleet was 2487 (OVL 496), a 1960 Bristol SC4LK 35-seat bodied bus. *G. Lumb*

21

Above:
Traditional and Elegant
Felix Motors Ltd, Hatfield near Doncaster, was using 8176 WY, a 1961 AEC
Regent V with Roe rear-entrance body on its Armthorpe service. *G. Lumb*

Right:
Another Football Special
T. Severn & Sons Ltd, Dunscroft, Doncaster, had this Leyland PD2/10,
KWW 514, with Roe body ready to work this special to the Rovers ground in
October 1964. *G. Lumb*

Above:
Premier
Harold Wilson Ltd from Stainforth, Doncaster, was using this 1954 Guy Arab double-deck bus, MWW 891, which had its Park Royal body finished by Guy Motors Ltd, on the Thorne service in March 1962.

24 *G. Lumb*

Right:
Not too Wide
Doncaster Corporation 130 (MDT 230) was one of 10 AEC Regent III type 9613A buses built in 1953 with 7ft 6in-wide Roe bodies and is seen at the old bus station at Glasgow Paddocks alongside an East Midland Motor Services Ltd Leyland Leopard, No L405, in May 1965. *G. Lumb*

Above:

Doncaster Pullman

Former Doncaster Corporation No 122 (KDT 393) was not five years old when sold to G. H. Ennifer, one of the Doncaster independents who traded as Blue Ensign and operated a joint service with East Midland, Rossie Motors and Doncaster Corporation to Rossington. This vehicle was used until July 1967 when it was sold via Norths dealer to a Nottingham PSV driving school. Fortunately it was bought for preservation by Tony Peart and is now restored to its original Doncaster livery.

G. Lumb

Above:
Fourth Option
Another independent to be seen on services to Rossington in June 1968 was KWT 600, a 1951 Daimler CVD6 which had a new Burlingham body fitted to it in 1954. This was operated by Rossie Motors (Rossington) Ltd on the joint service with Blue Ensign, East Midland and Doncaster Corporation between Doncaster and Rossington.
G. Lumb

Above:
Some Airmen Arrived by Bus
Leon Motor Services Ltd, Finningley, used this 1949 Daimler CVD6 with
Massey body on its services to and from Doncaster in March 1962, FBW 887
being a second-hand purchase in 1959. *G. Lumb*

Above:

United we Serve

Another Doncaster independent was United Services, the fleet name used by three operators — Bingley, Cooper and Everett — who jointly operated services between Doncaster and Wakefield. LTO 10 was a Daimler CVD6 with distinctive Duple lowbridge body was built in 1950 for Skill's, Nottingham, Bingleys purchasing it in 1954 for its share of United Services operations.

V. Nutton, Courtesy G. Lumb Collection

Right:
An Early Standee
The small BET fleet of Mexborough & Swinton
Traction Co Ltd started replacing its trolleybuses
between 1954 and 1961. No 51 was built in 1956
with a Weymann 34-seat bus body which had
accommodation for a further 29 standees and
was mounted on a Leyland Tiger Cub chassis.
G. Lumb

Far right:
London Exile
Seen leaving Wombwell for Rawmarsh, a village
near Rotherham, is a former London Transport
Daimler CWA6 utility bus, HGC 280, which had
been purchased in 1954 by Tom Burrows & Sons
who then rebodied it in 1957 with a new
Burlingham body.
V. Nutton, Courtesy G. Lumb Collection

Left:
Wartime Bristol
Another Tom Burrows & Sons vehicle, on its way from Rawmarsh to Leeds in May 1964, was No 50 (EWW 943), a 1945 utility Bristol K6A which had been rebodied with a new Burlingham body in 1957. *G. Lumb*

Above:
Variations in Livery
Rotherham Corporation was an avid user of Bristols. No 178 (EET 578), an East Lancashire-bodied Bristol K6B which was new in 1948, is seen in May 1962 with a similar 1947 Bristol No 169 (DET 373) in Rotherham town centre. *G. Lumb*

Left:
Next off
Rotherham Crossley No 214 (HET 514) was numerically the last Crossley bus in the Rotherham fleet, but when seen in Sheffield in 1966 was the first in the line-up for service 69 to Rotherham. Sister vehicle 213 was presented to the British Transport Commission for preservation, being the last double-deck Crossley to be built. *G. Lumb*

Above:
Rare Combination
This British Railways Board Leyland PD2/20 was fitted with an ECW highbridge body in 1957 and was painted in the livery of Sheffield Corporation which operated the 'C' fleet on behalf of British Railways. ECW and Bristol were state-owned at this time, and could only supply their products to the state sector. Thus the combination of Leyland and ECW at this period was very rare, and was only made possible at Sheffield by the railway involvement. No 3152 C is seen leaving Doncaster's South bus station in June 1968.

When Sheffield Corporation purchased the railway interests at the end of 1969 only four of the 'C' fleet were bought by the Corporation, all the others being dispersed to adjacent operators which still had railway interests, this one going to Yorkshire Woollen District. The platform doors had been fitted in 1963. *G. Lumb*

Left:
Sheffield Joint
British Transport Commission was the owner in 1959 of No 96B (KWE 796) which was also painted in Sheffield Corporation livery. It was allocated to the Joint Omnibus Committee 'B' fleet in which both partners, Sheffield Corporation and the railways, had 50% each. It was a 1948 AEC Regal I with a Weymann 34-seat rear-entrance body and it survived until 1961.
G. Lumb

Above:
Resting
Seen on the parking ground near to Pond Street bus station in October 1969 are three buses in Sheffield Corporation livery. They are No 1006 (5906 W), a 'B' fleet Burlingham-bodied Leyland Leopard type L1 new in 1960; No 1358 (658 BWB), a 'B' fleet Weymann-bodied Leyland Atlantean new in 1962; No 6 (6306 W), a Corporation-only 'A' fleet Weymann-bodied Leyland Leopard built in 1960. Prior to 1967 renumbering, No 1006 had been 1306 and No 6 had been 206. *G. Lumb*

Far left:
Rare Purchase
The wholly-owned Sheffield Corporation 'A' fleet contained a number of unusual vehicles including two Mann Egerton-bodied Leyland Titan PD2/12 buses supplied in 1952. They remained in service until 1965 shortly after this photograph was taken. *G. Lumb*

Left:
Unusual Route
One of the Sheffield Corporation routes ran an infrequent service up a private drive to a village whose origins lay with Sheffield Corporation Waterworks. No 830 (YWA 830) was one of 40 Roe-bodied Leyland PD2/20s purchased in 1957. It is seen approaching Ewden Village in 1970. *G. Lumb*

Above:

Independent Barred

A few miles north of Ewden is Deepcar, which was the terminus of Baddeley Bros Ltd's service from Huddersfield. Baddeley's had operated between Huddersfield and Sheffield for a short period before the implementation of the 1930 Road Traffic Act when it was forced to curtail it at Deepcar in 1932.

Leyland Tiger PS1 No 44 (GWY 77) was purchased in 1948 and had been fitted with a second-hand body. This in turn was replaced in 1954 by another second-hand body which was available when Yorkshire Woollen rebodied 24 single-deck buses with new double-deck bodies. It is seen in Holmfirth bus station on one of the routes to Penistone in October 1962. Holmfirth is now famous as the setting of the TV series 'Last of the Summer Wine'. *G. Lumb*

Right:

Rare Breed

Yorkshire Traction Co Ltd operated rural services into the Deepcar, Stocksbridge and Penistone areas. Seen at Thurgoland near Penistone in 1961 is Dennis Lancet No 867, new in 1950, with a Federation-style Brush body. It survived until 1962. *G. Lumb*

Far left:
Starting a New Life
Yorkshire Traction Co Ltd No 1192H started life in 1950 as CHE 857, a Leyland Tiger PS2/3 fitted with a Windover coach body (similar to the Cherry's example shown earlier). In 1961 it was fitted with a new Roe 63-seat highbridge body, hence the 'H', and new registration VHE 192.
G. Lumb

Left:
Overweight
During the summer of 1968, Hebble Motor Services, unable to use heavy buses over the North Bridge at Halifax, borrowed four Leyland 56-seat buses from Yorkshire Traction, at the same time sending on loan four 70-seat AEC Regent V buses it could not use, to Barnsley. Hebble 306 (JCP 672) is seen in Barnsley bus station. This vehicle had started life as Hebble 304 in 1958 and had to be rebuilt in 1958 after overturning at speed on North Bridge, Halifax. It became 306 on return to Hebble from Metro-Cammell.
V. Nutton, Courtesy G. Lumb Collection

Below left:
Sure as the Sunrise
South Yorkshire Motors Ltd from Pontefract operated a network of services linking Pontefract with Leeds, Doncaster, Barnsley and Selby. The company had a particular liking for Albions and the last double-deck Albion CX37 to be purchased was No 72 (JWR 875) which had a Strachan 55-seat lowbridge body fitted when new in 1950. It is seen at Barnsley bus station.
V. Nutton, Courtesy G. Lumb Collection

Right:
Seaside Exile
A. Rowe & Sons (Cudworth) Ltd operated this 1951 Leyland PD2/12 which had an East Lancashire Coach Builders body, built originally for Ribble Motor Services Ltd's 'White Lady' fleet. DCK 216 is seen at Royston station in 1964. *G. Lumb*

Far right:
Ideal Partnership
Ideal Motor Services was a partnership between Robert Taylor & Sons of Cudworth and H. Wray & Sons, Hoyle Mill. H. Wray operated KHE 526 which was rebuilt in 1956 with a new Roe body. It had started life as a 1947 Leyland PS1 single-deck coach. *G. Lumb*

Left:

Only Very Early Risers Caught the First Bus at 1.50am

J. W. Mosley & Sons, Barugh Green, used this former Sheffield Corporation Daimler CWD6 No 518 which had been rebodied in 1953 with a new Roe body. It was used until January 1965 on Mosley's service from Higham to Barnsley. *G. Lumb*

Above:

Not a Record

In 1958, Larratt Pepper & Sons Ltd, Thurnscoe, purchased an Albion Aberdonian type MR11 with a 45-seat Plaxton bus body for its service from Barnsley to Thurnscoe. It was numbered 19 (WWX 478) and was used until January 1973. *G. Lumb*

Above:

Bretton Interchange

County Motors (Lepton) Ltd was taken over by Yorkshire Traction on 1 January 1969. This view of Bretton Crossroads in late-1968 shows the various services which connected, giving interchange facilities between the Huddersfield, Wakefield and Barnsley services. The short single-decker, a Leyland Tiger Cub, was provided on Saturdays to duplicate the Wakefield end of the service to and from Bretton. *G. Lumb*

Above:
Only Part BET
County Motors (Lepton) Ltd was jointly owned by West Riding Automobile Co Ltd (an independent until 1968), Yorkshire Woollen District Transport Co Ltd and Yorkshire Traction Co Ltd. In 1961, County purchased two Guy Wulfrunian double-deck buses for its direct service to Wakefield. County Motors, a 25-vehicle fleet, had problems with maintaining them and the last day they were used was Sunday 28 April 1963, the vehicles being transferred to West Riding on the following day. They are seen at Flockton on their last day in service.
G. Lumb

49

Above:
Tramway Replacements were Red
West Riding Automobile Co Ltd, Wakefield, was formed in 1922 to operate
motorbuses on behalf of the Yorkshire (West Riding) Electric Tramways Co Ltd
which had operated tramways since 1904. West Riding omnibuses were painted
green and when the tramways were abandoned in 1932 they were replaced by
50 buses painted red having Roe centre-entrance double-deck bodies. These
were replaced after the war with similar bodied AECs. No 111 was a 1949
example and is seen shortly after withdrawal in Leeds in 1965. *G. Lumb*

Right:
Satisfied Customer
Yorkshire Woollen District Transport Co Ltd purchased 35 Guy Arabs between
1942 and 1945. These were followed by a further 10 Guy Arab IIs in 1946 which
received Roe bodies. No 519 (HD 7652) is seen waiting to leave the Rosemary
Lane terminus in Huddersfield for Bradford.
R. Brook

Above:
First of the Big Single-Deckers
Yorkshire Woollen District Transport Co Ltd Leyland Royal Tiger No 693 was one of five fitted with
42-seat Brush bodies. It is seen leaving Mirfield in July 1963 on the Wakefield to Cullingworth service
which Yorkshire worked jointly with West Riding. *G. Lumb*

Above:

New Lease of Life

Yorkshire Woollen District Transport Co Ltd Leyland Tiger PS2 No 721 was delivered as a 32-seat bus in 1950. In 1955 its chassis was lengthened and the seating capacity of its Willowbrook body was increased to 38, with its livery being changed to cream for summer services. *V. Nutton, Courtesy G. Lumb Collection*

J. WOOD

MIRFIELD
VIA
KNOWLE

CROSSLEY

EVD 406

Left:
Woods Liked Crossleys
Joseph Wood & Son, Mirfield, was one of three operators to operate independently from different termini in Dewsbury via Knowl to Mirfield. Woods purchased its first double-deck bus from Baxter, Airdrie, in 1953 and fitted a new 56-seat Roe body before it entered service in August 1953. It is seen at the Woods terminus in Dewsbury in 1963.
G. Lumb

Above:
Early Underfloor
J. J. Longstaff & Sons Ltd also participated in this service to Mirfield and in early 1962 at the Dewsbury terminus OUP 579, a Sentinel STC 4 with Sentinel body, is ready to depart to Mirfield. Longstaffs purchased it second-hand from Phillips of Glynceiriog in late 1961 and sold it in late 1965 to another Phillips, at Shiptonthorpe.
G. Lumb

Joint Purchase
Huddersfield Joint Omnibus Committee, a joint
operation between Huddersfield Corporation and
British Railways, purchased a fleet of 30 Daimler
CVG6 single-deck buses with 34-seat Willowbrook
bodies after the war. No 79 (DVH 119) was new in
1948. *G. Lumb*

Winter Problem
Huddersfield Joint Omnibus Committee also
purchased a number of AEC Regent III double-
deck buses with Park Royal or East Lancs
highbridge bodies. No 175, a 1951 example, with
8ft-wide bodywork was in difficulties in January
1963 whilst attempting to reach Scapegoat Hill.
G. Lumb

Left:

A Famous Name

Hanson Buses Ltd rebuilt a number of former AEC Regal III buses and coaches and fitted them with new 39-seat Roe forward-entrance bodies. No 360 was one of three rebuilt in 1960 and is seen working one of the joint Colne Valley services which it shared with Huddersfield Joint Omnibus Committee. It is seen approaching Wilberlee a few days before Huddersfield purchased both Hansons and the railway interests in Huddersfield Joint Omnibus Committee. *G. Lumb*

Above:

Still White Rose Country

Before the 1974 boundary changes, the West Riding of Yorkshire stretched west over the Pennines to the outskirts of Oldham. This area included the Saddleworth district where the principal services were operated by the North Western Road Car Co Ltd with the municipalities of Oldham, Manchester and SHMD (Stalybridge, Hyde, Mossley & Dukinfield Transport & Electricity Board) providing others, often on a joint basis with North Western Road Car Co. Hansons also linked Huddersfield with Oldham. This view shows Oldham 107, a Leyland PD3 *en route* to Manchester, whilst a North Western Alexander-bodied AEC Reliance heads towards Uppermill. *G. Lumb*

Above:
One Man Solution
Halifax Corporation operated motorbuses both for the Corporation and for the Halifax Joint Omnibus Committee which was 50% owned by British Railways. For the joint 'B' fleet, when faced with rising costs and falling receipts on rural services, 14 of the early postwar AEC Regal single-deck buses were rebuilt with forward entrances. By modifying the front bulkhead they could be used for one man operation, 266 being converted in 1953.

V. Nutton, Courtesy G. Lumb Collection

Above:

These Could Motor

Halifax purchased six Daimler export model CD650 buses with East Lancs bodies for the Corporation-owned 'A' fleet. The 10.6 litre engine gave a lively performance on the Halifax hills. No 83 (CCP 603) is seen at Ainley Top after climbing up from Elland in October 1961 on its way to Huddersfield. *G. Lumb*

Right:
Duplicate Fleet
Todmorden JOC, a Joint Corporation and railway operator, was unusual in following railway practice with some vehicles being given an 'X' prefix fleet number indicating that they were on the duplicate list. X24 was one of two which survived as spare vehicles from 1951 to 1960/61 when new Nos 23 and 24 were supplied. X24 was owned by British Railways when seen in 1960 outside Millwood Depot.
V. Nutton, Courtesy G. Lumb Collection

Far right:
Another Football Special
Todmorden for many years had a very standardised fleet: 40 Leyland Titan double-deck buses, all having Leyland lowbridge bodywork. No 23 was one of the last ones to be supplied in 1951 and was owned by Todmorden Corporation. It is seen in 1961 about to leave Todmorden for Burnley's football ground. *G. Lumb*

Above:

Brief Encounter

Hebble Motor Services Ltd with depots in Halifax and Bradford operated the railways' 'C' fleet services in the Halifax area, linking Leeds with Burnley and Rochdale as well as local services to Bingley, Wyke and Huddersfield. One infrequent local service was from Mountain to Harecroft via Queensbury. In July 1967, AEC Reliance No 195 (PCP 803) with a 43-seat Alexander body had had an argument with something. The company's tow wagon, a former bus, had just arrived to sort it out!

G. Lumb

Above:
Another Cross-Border Service
A number of Burnley, Colne & Nelson Joint Omnibus Committee routes extended into the Craven District of the West Riding. No 161, a Leyland PD1 built in 1947 with 56-seat Weymann body, is seen loading at Waller Hill bus station, Skipton, prior to returning to Colne in October 1961. *G. Lumb*

Far left:
Railway Feeder

R & M of Slaidburn trading as Bounty Motor Services was operating two services from Clitheroe station to Slaidburn using Seddon FBD 448 which is seen outside Clitheroe railway station in May 1962. Unable to make ends meet, it sold the service to Leedhams of Dunsop Bridge in July 1965.
G. Lumb

Left:
Dale Bus Service

J. Cowgill & Sons, Lothersdale, was the proud owner of Albion LWR 762 in July 1965. It was used on a service between Colne and Crosshills via Lothersdale until May 1967 when the service was withdrawn.
G. Lumb

Below left:
Service in Transit

Ezra Laycock Ltd, based at Barnoldswick, was using Leyland FV 5734 in October 1961 on its service from Skipton's Waller Hill bus station to Bradley, which had been acquired from Silver Star Motor Services in August 1961. In early 1963, Laycocks passed the Bradley service to West Yorkshire Road Car. Laycocks continued to operate Skipton to Carleton and Skipton to Barnoldswick until August 1972 when the business was sold to Pennine Motor Services from Gargrave.

One of Laycock's AEC Monocoach buses is seen behind the Leyland.
G. Lumb

Above:
Pennine Survivor
Pennine Motor Services operated a number of services extending northwest of Skipton. JWT 724, a 1950 Leyland PS2/1 with a 35-seat Burlingham body, is seen at Gargrave in October 1961. *G. Lumb*

Right:
A Proper Rural Bus
In May 1967, Hillcrest Coaches (Settle) Ltd was using a Leyland Comet CPO1 with a 33-seat Bellhouse Hartwell body on the service from Settle to Horton-in-Ribblesdale which connected with Pennine's trunk route from Skipton. *G. Lumb*

but it's cheaper by bus

22

KEIGHLEY - WEST YORKSHIRE

KDG 16

BWY 994

CARLING LAGER BEER

Left:
Duke of Devonshire Outpost
Keighley-West Yorkshire Services Ltd was a company jointly owned by
Keighley Corporation and West Yorkshire Road Car Co Ltd, the latter operating
it from its inception in 1932. Typical of the early 1960s fleet are KDG16, a 1937
Bristol K5G rebodied by Roe in 1950, and KDB13, a 1948 Bristol K6B with ECW
body, which are seen in Keighley. *G. Lumb*

Above:
Perkins Power
West Yorkshire Road Car Co purchased a number of Bristol SUL4A single-deck
buses fitted with 36-seat ECW bodies for its rural services. One of these,
SMA17, was fitted with a Perkins six-cylinder engine, in place of the standard
four-cylinder Albion, in 1966 and renumbered SMP17. It is seen in Haworth
returning from Stanbury in August 1969 on a Keighley-West Yorkshire route
which had been acquired from the Brontë Bus Co in January 1956. *G. Lumb*

Left:
First Postwar
Bradford Corporation's first postwar motorbuses to be delivered were the
20 AEC Regent III 0961s with Northern Coach Builders bodies which entered
service in late-1947 and early-1948. Two examples are seen in 1961 passing each
other on the Bierley Route. *G. Lumb*

Above:
Yorkshire Tyke
Samuel Ledgard, Armley, Leeds, purchased two Guy Arabs in late 1945. Both
were rebodied in 1951 with new Roe double-deck bodies. JUA 762 is seen on the
Leeds to Bradford service climbing the hill into Pudsey in 1960.
G. Lumb

73

Above:
Reversed Registration
One of Ledgards' original vehicles was a Karrier purchased in 1914 with registration No U 1949. In 1957 Ledgards purchased six new AEC

Regent V 65-seat Roe-bodied double-deck buses. The first one was registered 1949 U and is seen awaiting dispatch from the Roe works at Crossgates, Leeds.
Roe, Courtesy G. Lumb Collection

Above:
Not Blue for Long
In October 1967, Samuel Ledgards was purchased by the West Yorkshire Road Car Co Ltd with some services being immediately resold to Leeds Corporation or Leeds and Bradford Corporations jointly. Of the vehicles taken over, only 14 were operated by West Yorkshire Road Car Co. Two of these are seen in Otley bus station in October 1967 before repainting into West Yorkshire Road Car Co livery. They are former South Wales Regent V DAW3 (NCY 453) and 1953 U new to Ledgards Regent V, now West Yorkshire Road Car Co DAW9.
G. Lumb

Left:

Tilling Standard

Typical of the early postwar fleet of West Yorkshire Road Car Co Ltd was No 255 which was a 1950 Bristol L5G with 35-seat ECW body. It was renumbered SG134 in 1954 and is seen in 1960 at Bradford's Chester Street bus station. *V. Nutton, Courtesy G. Lumb Collection*

Above:

Not to be Repeated

Leeds Corporation supported the local bodybuilder C. H. Roe for a large proportion of its fleet. In 1949 after Roe became part of the ACV group which included Park Royal, Roe built a solitary example to Park Royal design for Leeds on an AEC Regent III 9612E chassis. It remained the sole example to be built by Roe to this design. No 450 is seen in Infirmary Street, Leeds, in September 1964. *G. Lumb*

Right:
Sale Promotional
Leeds Corporation purchased 30 Daimler CVG6LX/30 double-deck buses in 1959 which were fitted with attractive 70-seat Roe bodies. In April 1962 the first of the 30, No 502, was loaned to Huddersfield Corporation for evaluation for both trolleybus replacements for the Corporation fleet or for the Huddersfield Joint Omnibus Committee fleet. It is seen at Golcar on a Joint Omnibus Committee route. Both fleets, satisfied with its performance, took delivery in 1964 of examples fitted with forward-entrance bodies by Roe.
G. Lumb

Below right:
No, It's not Tony driving!
The York Pullman Bus Co Ltd operated a network of services based on York. They filled many of the gaps left by the major companies. This fine shot shows No 65 (JDN 669), a 1954 AEC Regent III type 6812A, climbing to go over the main railway line north of York in 1966. Sister vehicle No 64 was bought by Tony Peart for preservation.
V. Nutton, Courtesy G. Lumb Collection

Above:
Leeds Independents
Kippax & District Motor Co Ltd and Farsley Omnibus Co Ltd were among companies taken over by Wallace Arnold Tours in the 1950s. MUM 461 started life as a Daimler CVD6 coach with Farsley Omnibus, being rebodied in 1956 with a Roe double-deck body. In March 1958 it was transferred to Kippax & District where it remained until 30 March 1968 when both Farsley and Kippax services were sold to Leeds Corporation. It is seen outside Ledston Luck Colliery in April 1962.
G. Lumb